Introduction

This guide covers the old Scottish counties of Peebles and Selkirk plus a part of the southern end of the old county of Lanarkshire (*see* centre pages for map). The landscape is one of long, flat-bottomed valleys winding through a mass of low, rounded hills. With the exception of forestry plantations (*Walk 21*), the hills are largely bare. The highest peak, Broad Law *(19)* rises to 2,760ft/840m.

The largest town in the area is Lanark. This sits on the River Clyde, and there are fine paths through the woods by the Falls of Clyde east of the old industrial model town of New Lanark *(2)*. South of this the land becomes more rural, and there is a quiet circuit from the small town of Douglas *(1)*, plus a climb up the isolated peak of Tinto Hill *(4)*. The other significant settlement in the west of the area is the handsome old country town of Biggar. Just to the east of this is the village of Broughton, from where there is a climb to a fine viewpoint in the Broughton Heights *(5)*.

To the north of this, the area includes the southern end of the Pentland Hills (*see* companion guide *Walks Edinburgh* for routes in the northern part of the range). There are a number of good paths through these hills, and a circuit is included from the little village of West Linton *(3)*.

In the eastern half of the area the population is small, and largely concentrated in or around the valley of the River Tweed, which runs 97 miles from its source in the hills north of Moffat to Berwick on the North Sea coast. The major towns and service centres are the old county towns of Peebles and Selkirk, which have populations of around 10 thousand and five thousand respectively. East and south of the Tweed the hills become higher, the valleys longer and more winding. Historically, this was 'reiver' country: the lawless land of cattle thieves and brigands which existed on either side of the Scotland/England border before the union of the two countries. Throughout this area you will see a number

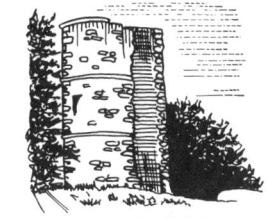

Castle Douglas (Walk 1)

of castles and towers which serve as a reminder of this turbulent period.

In Peebles, there are walks along the banks of the Tweed (passing the dramatic Neidpath Castle) *(6)*, onto the surrounding hills *(7)* and through the dense conifer plantations of Glentress Forest *(10)*, plus a short climb through woodland to a viewpoint on the remains of an Iron Age fort *(9)* and a loop up a short glen *(11)*.

A short way down the Tweed valley you reach the old mill town of Innerleithen, from where there is a straight climb to the peak of Lee Pen *(12)*. South from here, across the river, you pass the historic Traquair House, just beyond which a side road leads to the start of a circuit up a pleasant valley then back across the hilltops *(13)*.

East again, near the junction of the roads to Galashiels and Selkirk, is the village of Clovenfords, once famous for its grapes, where there is a circuit over a low, grassy hill *(14)*. South from here is the town of Selkirk, in the valley of the Ettrick Water. Near here there are three routes: two hill climbs onto the ridge on the north side of the valley of the Yarrow Water *(15,17)* and a circuit through the grounds of Bowhill Estate, passing the main house and the ruin of Newark Castle *(16)*.

To the west there are two further routes. In the valley of the Ettrick Water there is a rough circuit through the bleak grazing lands of these higher hills *(20)*. In the valley of the Yarrow Water there is a path around St Mary's Loch – the largest natural loch in the Scottish borders *(18)*. A feature of both these walks are monuments to the writer James Hogg – also known as 'The Ettrick Shepherd' (1770-1835). More generally, memorials to local writers – such as the statue of Sir Walter Scott outside the Clovenfords Hotel *(14)* – are common in this area. Perhaps the most relevant to walkers will be the John Buchan Way *(8)*; a 13 mile/21km waymarked route linking Peebles and Broughton, named after the famous novelist.

There is some wonderful walking in this area, and we hope this guide will provide you with a good introduction.

James Hogg Monument (Walk 18)

1 Douglas_____B

A circuit through parkland, farmland and woodland, passing a fine old church and the remains of a ruined castle. Paths good throughout.
Length: **4 miles/6.5km**; Height Climbed: **170ft/50m**.

O.S. Sheet 72

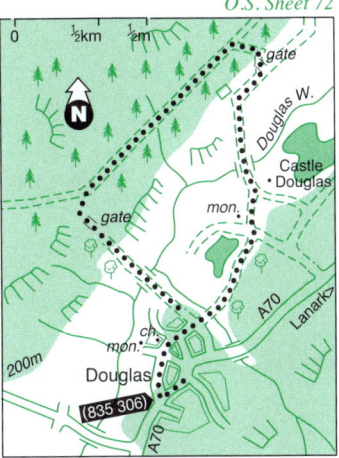

Douglas, 12 miles south of Lanark on the A70, is a village with strong historical links with the Douglas family. This walk passes through the neighbouring Douglas Estate.

Park in Douglas and walk down Main St, running north from the main road. At a junction bear right, passing to the right of the semi-ruined St Bride's Church (mausoleum of the Lords of Douglas). At the next junction bear left (signposted for 'Castle Dangerous') to reach the entrance gate to the estate.

Keep straight on at the junction immediately beyond the gate and follow the driveway through parkland, up the side of a small lake. At the end of the lake the track splits. Go left.

A rough track heads left, down the far side of the lake, but for this route keep to the main track, passing the monument to the disbanding of The Cameronians (a regiment first raised in the village) and continuing to a T-junction.

For this walk you will go left, but first keep straight on to visit the remains – part of a single tower – of Castle Douglas (also known as Castle Dangerous).

The track crosses a bridge over the Douglas Water then continues to a house on the edge of woodland, where it turns right. In a short distance, go through a gate to the left and take a track into the trees.

Follow this track round a hairpin bend and up to a T-junction. Go left and follow a straight track through the trees for a little under a mile/1.6km, until it swings hard right. At this point keep straight on, along a rough path; crossing a mound then descending to the corner of a field.

Edge left, parallel to the field to your left, to reach a gate. Go through this and follow a line of trees down to a bridge; cross this and keep straight on to return to the gate into the estate.

When returning, keep right at the church on a metalled track to visit the fine statue of the Earl of Angus – the founder of the Cameronians.

2 Falls of Clyde & New Lanark — B

A popular riverside walk, starting at the splendid old mill town of New Lanark then following good paths through woodland and past waterfalls. Length: **4 miles/6.5km**; *Height Climbed:* undulating.

O.S. Sheet 72

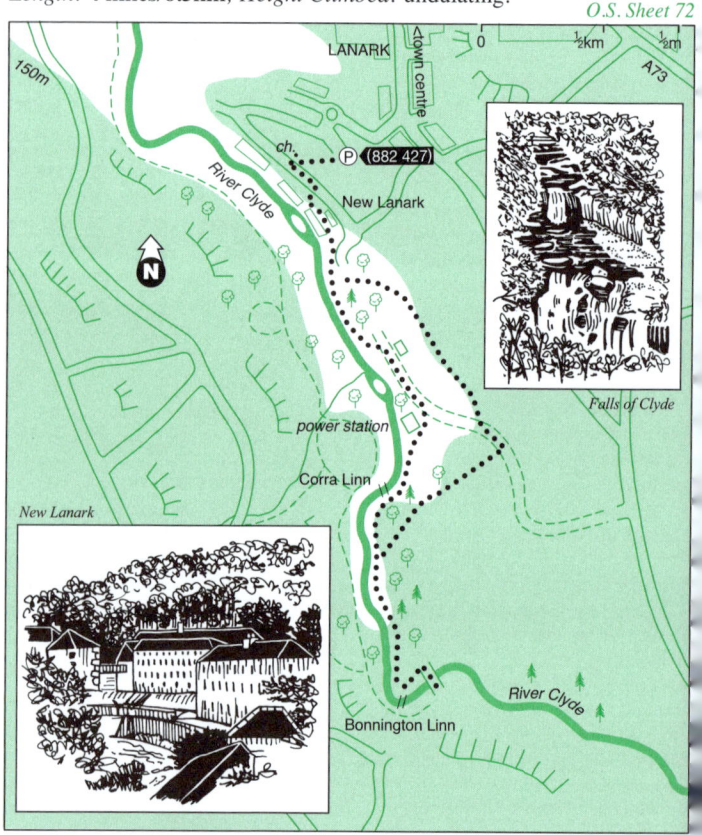

Falls of Clyde

New Lanark

New Lanark – a planned, 19th-century, industrial village – is one of the finest visitor attractions in this area.

It was built to house workers for a cotton mill powered by the waters of the Clyde. Over 2,000 people lived or worked in the village, and it was a hugely important example of industrial urban planning. The riverside mill and terraces are well worth a visit on their own account. In addition, they provide a good start point for this fine riverside walk.

To reach the village, follow the signs south from the A73/Wellgatehead, near the centre of Lanark. At junctions, follow the signs for the visitor car park.

Cross the road from the car park and follow the path signposted for the village; down and across the slope to join a metalled road by the church. A sign points left for Falls of Clyde. After a short distance there is a gateway to your right. Go through this and keep straight on, down the steps to the right of the Visitor Attraction Centre. At the bottom of the steps go left, now with the mill lade to your left. Beyond the old school the road splits. Keep straight on (left) to reach a stone arch at the start of the walk.

There are two signposted paths through the wooded Falls of Clyde Wildlife Reserve: the red marked Clyde Walkway and the blue marked Woodland Trail. This walk uses both of these routes.

Both walks start along the riverside path, and from the very beginning you are walking through fine mature woodland with falls and weirs in the river down to your right. After a short distance a clear path heads off to the left, marked by a sign showing three wavy blue lines. That is your return route; for now, keep straight on along the clear path.

A little further on the path joins a metalled road. This quickly reaches a hydroelectric power station then turns away from the river. Leave the road to the right at this point (sign), following a track to the left of the power station then continuing along a clear path.

Just beyond the falls at Corra Linn the blue route cuts off back-left. That is your return route, but for now continue by the river up to the bridge above Bonnington Linn. There are paths down the far side of the river, but no easy loop, so double back from this point.

Return to the junction and go ahead-right, now on the blue route. The path passes the remains of an old walled garden to the right, then continues, passing a fine roofless folly (the Bonnington Pavilion, an early camera obscura) and hydro workings to reach a kissing-gate, beyond which a clear, straight track runs through an open grazing area.

At the far end of the track a second gate leads on to a metalled road. Turn left, descending into woodland. After a short distance there is a gap to your right and a sign for the blue route. Turn off here and follow a narrow track along the top of the trees, with a field to your right and the river audible below.

Continue until a sign for the blue route points left, off the track. Follow a path downhill to rejoin the route at the junction noted before. Turn right to return to the start.

3 West Linton _____A

A complex circuit over the open moor and through farmland. Paths are generally clear, but part of the route will require some navigation. Beautiful moorland landscape and fine views. Be careful to avoid grazing cattle around Garvald. Length: **11 miles/18km**; Height Climbed: **490ft/150m**.

O.S. Sheet 72

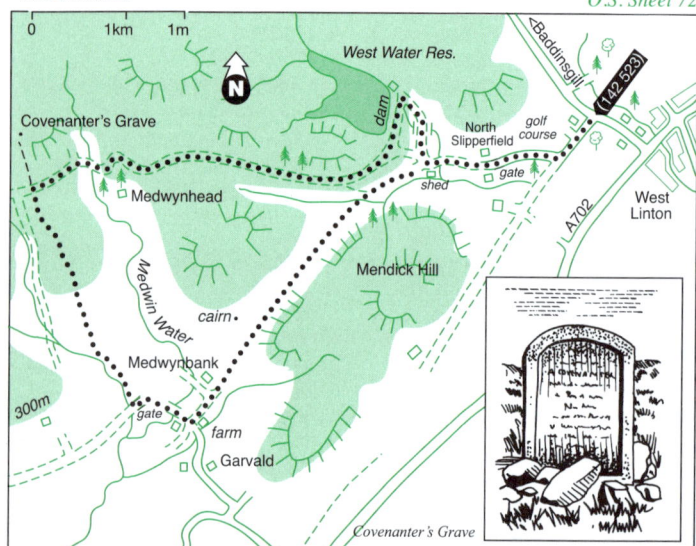

Covenanter's Grave

West Linton is a small village, 19 miles south-west of Edinburgh on the A702. In the village, turn off the main road onto the minor road signposted for Baddinsgill. In half a mile a minor road heads left, signposted for the golf club and the right of way to Crosswood. There is limited roadside parking here. If that is not possible, you will need to park in West Linton and add another mile/1.6km to the route.

Walk on along the road, passing through the golf course (watch out for errant shots!). At a signposted junction keep right (Crosswood) – ie, on the metalled road – and continue until you go through a gate level with the end of the golf course then pass to the left of a group of houses.

After a short distance you cross the little West Water. Immediately beyond a track cuts off to the left, to a shed. Ignore this and climb up to a signposted junction. The track straight ahead (Garvald) is your return route, but for now keep climbing to the right (Crosswood).

After a short distance a third track heads off to the left. Ignore this and continue on the metalled track, climbing up to the right-hand end of the dam over West Water Reservoir.

Cross the dam. At the far end, ignore a faint track climbing to the right and follow the main track down to a junction with another track. Turn right along this.

Follow this clear track for 2 miles/3km (junctions with smaller paths/tracks are marked by arrows). There is a line of confers up to your right at first, then the track descends towards the little wood around Medwynhead. The track passes to the right of the wood then zig-zags down to cross Medwin Water in a deep little glen.

Ignore the track heading right, beyond the river, and climb the far side of the glen, then continue to reach a signposted four-way junction on the moor. It is worth making a short climb to the right at this point (Crosswood) to enjoy the views and to visit a gravestone marking the grave of a 17th-century Covenanter. The path is faint but the route is marked by posts. Having done so, return to the signpost and go south, off the track (Dolphinton).

There is no clear path, but if you look across the moor you should be able to pick out a tall post with a yellow top. A series of eight of these posts leads you a little over a mile/1.6km across the moor. If you get lost, aim to join the West Water (the burn off to your right) just as it enters fields. At this point the path drops into the glen to follow the burn.

The path climbs to run by a fence then descends to a signposted junction with a sunken track. Go left (West Linton), through a gate. After 40 paces an arrow points ahead-right, down to a footbridge over the Medwin Water. Cross the footbridge, and a stile immediately beyond, then walk along the edge of a narrow field with a fence to your right.

Go through a metal gate, just before the buildings at Garvald Home Farm, then immediately go left on a short path which quickly leads you to the junction of vehicle tracks in the middle of the farm. Go left here, with the farmhouse to your right.

This is the entrance drive to Medwynbank. Just before the house, a track heads off to the left. Ignore this and keep straight on between gateposts. A second track goes right, on the near side of a small pond. Ignore this and keep straight on, between the pond and the house. When the track swings left, into the house, keep straight on on a rough track leading to a gate into a field.

Walk on with a stand of conifers to you right, passing through two further gates to reach the open, grassy moor. Beyond the end of the trees (note the fine burial cairn, ahead-left) continue along a rough track in the same direction for a little over a mile/1.6km, ignoring tracks to your right, to return to the junction passed before.

Turn right to return to the start.

4 Tinto Hill _____ B

A straightforward, classic, popular hill climb on good paths. No doubt about the route and excellent views. Length: **4 miles/6.5km** *(there and back); Height Climbed:* **1,550ft/480m**.

O.S. Sheet 72

Tinto Hill, 4 miles south-west of Biggar, is one of the primary landmarks of the region: an isolated peak rising to 2,333ft/711m, topped by a large Bronze Age cairn. The climb is enjoyable, but the main attraction of the walk is the view, so make sure you pick a clear day. Also, ideally, go on a week day, as this is a very popular climb on weekends.

To reach the start, drive south from Biggar on the A702, quickly turning west on the A72/73 road for Lanark. The car park for the walk is signposted to the left at a four-way junction.

The climb requires no description: just start along the clear path from the back of the car park and follow it to the top. Near the start you will pass the grass-covered mounds of an Iron Age fort.

The weather will dictate how far you can see from the top, but the hill's isolated position means the views are excellent in all directions. On a clear day you may see as far as the Lake District peaks to the south and the hills of Arran to the west.

Return by the same route.

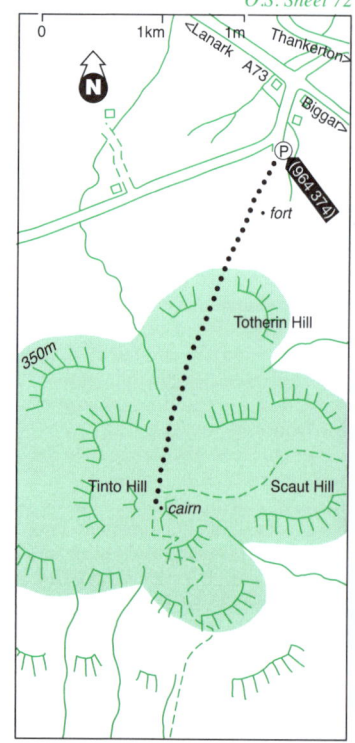

Tinto Hill from the South-East

5 Broughton Heights _____ A

A lineal hill climb on good paths, leading to a terrific view. Choose a clear day. Length: **6 miles/9km** (there and back); *Height Climbed:* **950ft/290m**.

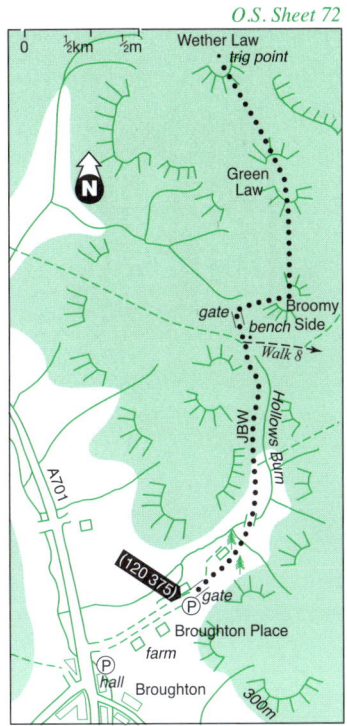

O.S. Sheet 72

The little village of Broughton sits at the junction of the A701 and the B7016, 5 miles east of Biggar. Immediately to the north of the village a metalled driveway heads east, off the A701, signposted for Broughton Place. Follow this drive up to the buildings at Broughton Place farm. Pass to the left of these then continue, passing a large baronial house, to reach a car park by a cottage at the end of the road. (**NB:** If this is full, go back to Broughton and park behind the village hall. This adds 2 miles/3.2km to the walk.)

Go through a gate at the top of the car park (for this section of the climb you are on the John Buchan Way – see Walk 8). The track beyond splits immediately. Keep right, walking up the side of a glen with a fence to your right. The track passes between small conifer plantations then slants across the slope to cross Hollows Burn on a footbridge.

The track beyond runs up the left-hand side of the glen. (A couple of paths head off to the right, to climb Hammer Head, but for this route stick to the main path.)

You climb to a bench. A sign points right for the JBW, but for this walk go left, on a fainter path, climbing to a fence on the ridge, which you should join at a gate/stile.

Cross the stile and turn right, on a rough path, with the fence to your right. On the main ridge there is a junction of fences. Go left, following the line of the fence up the ridge.

Continue until you reach the trig point – the views are magnificent in every direction – then return by the same route.

6 Tweed Walk _____ B/C

A series of linked footpaths, tracks and quiet public roads by the banks of the River Tweed, through woodland and farmland, passing Neidpath Castle. The route can be walked in its entirety, or shortened at three points. Length: **1½-7 miles/2.5-11km**; Height Climbed: undulating.

O.S. Sheet 73

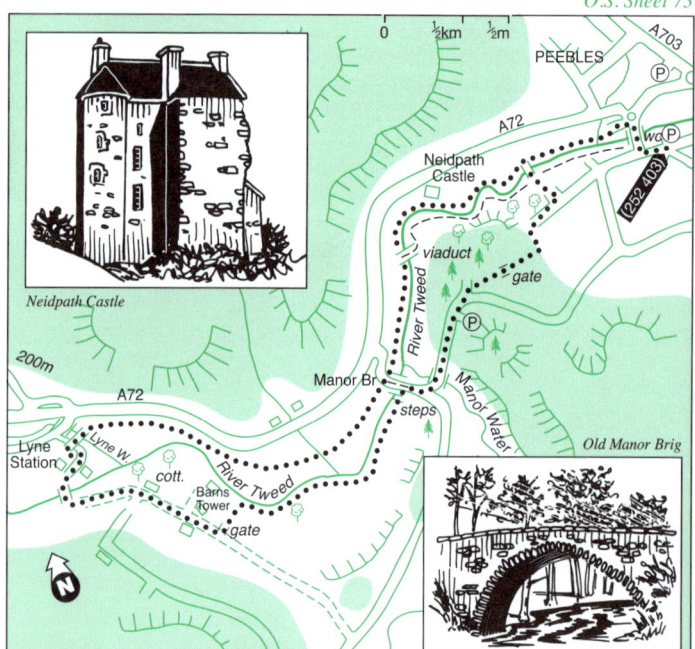

To reach Kingsmeadow car park in Peebles, drive/walk west along the High Street to reach a roundabout in front of a church. Turn left here, over the bridge over the River Tweed. The car park is to your left after a short distance.

Walk back across the bridge and turn left, down the road on the near side of the Bridge Inn. Pass to the left of the swimming pool and walk on along the river, crossing the end of a small river (Eddleston Water).

When the buildings end you continue through Hay Lodge Park, passing a footbridge over the river.

(**For the shortest circuit**, cross this bridge and turn left.)

At the end of the park there is a signposted junction. Keep straight on (Lyne) on a rough path. The riverside path passes below the splendid old tower house of Neidpath Castle and continues to reach the viaduct which once carried the railway over the river. **For a return from this point**, climb onto the viaduct and turn left, over the river. On the far side, turn left and follow the rough riverside path back to the start. **For the longer routes**, pass under the viaduct and continue.

The riverside path eventually climbs up to join the old railway. Continue along this, with Manor Bridge (a road bridge) visible ahead. When you reach the road you have a choice. **A turn to the left at this point**, over the bridge, will give a shorter version of this walk (*see map*); simply follow the description for the end of the long circuit from here. **Otherwise**, cross the road and climb steps to rejoin the railway.

Continue on this straightforward path for 1½ miles/2.5km until it crosses the Lyne Water and the minor road just beyond. Immediately beyond this, turn left (yellow arrow) and a flight of steps leads down to the road. Turn right along this (signposted for Peebles), and follow the road through houses and down to its end by the river. A path quickly leads to a footbridge over the river. Cross this and turn left.

The path pulls away from the river, through trees, and passes to the right of a cottage (Millbraehead). Here there is a junction. Ignore the track to the right and keep straight on, between gate posts. A straight driveway leads between the pink-harled Barns Tower and a group of other buildings and continues.

After a further 300 paces you reach a signposted junction. Go left here (Tweed Walk), through a gate, and walk down a grassy track with a wall to your left. You rejoin the river and continue beside it, back down to Manor Bridge.

Climb the steps on the near side of the bridge and turn right along the minor road. After 100 paces there is a junction. Go left here, follow the old road over Old Manor Brig (1702) then climb the slope beyond to reach a car park and viewpoint.

Continue along the road for a short distance, until the trees end to your left. At this point a right of way sign points left. Follow this into the trees.

The path leads down to a gate/stile leading into a field. Go down the right-hand side of the field (green arrow), with Peebles visible below. At the end of the field there is a further gate, leading into a lane between fences. Follow this down to join the end of a road through new houses.

Continue down the road until a sign points left for the riverside paths. Walk down through the industrial estate to reach the footbridge over the river leading back to Hay Lodge Park.

Cross the river here and retrace your steps.

7 Cademuir Hill _____ B

Two forest walks which climb to a fine, open ridge walk, leading to Iron Age forts and terrific views. Length: **5 miles/8km**; Height Climbed: **980ft/300m**.

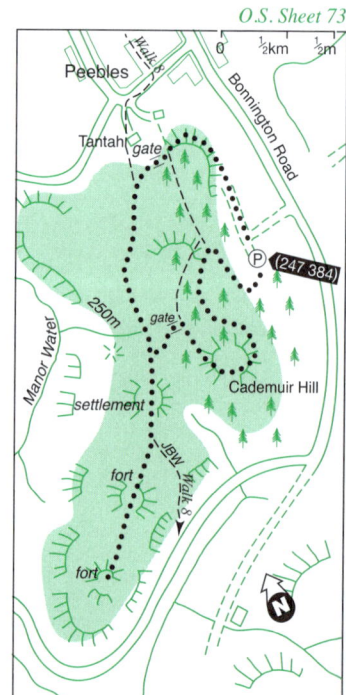

O.S. Sheet 73

To reach the start of this walk, drive south across the bridge over the Tweed in Peebles then turn second right (Springhill Rd). Immediately before the tennis courts turn right onto Springwood Rd, then first left onto Bonnington Rd. Follow this narrow road for a mile, out of the houses, until the signposted entrance to Cademuir appears to your right.

Drive up the straight drive then turn left, into the car park. To start this route, walk back to the top of the drive and keep straight on along a clear path (red/blue waymarks).

The path is straight at first, with fields down to your right, then it swings left and climbs. At a four-way junction keep straight on to reach a stile/gate leading into a narrow field, with a house to your right.

Look for the path heading left, up the middle of this rough grazing field. At first, this is signposted as the John Buchan Way. Beyond the grassy mounds of the first ancient settlement, the JBW heads off to the left, beside a field wall. At this point you keep straight on, up the ridge, to reach the remains of the fort on the peak of the ridge. Continue to the next peak to reach a smaller, but more distinct, circle of walls. The views are splendid.

Double back along the ridge. Ahead-right you will see the bald head of Cademuir Hill rising above the conifers. Near the first settlement, take a rough path which climbs to your right to join the wall around the trees. Look for a metal gate in this wall and go through it.

Beyond the gate you are immediately on a waymarked path. Go right and follow the red markers back to the car park.

8 The John Buchan Way ———————————————A

A waymarked path through hill country, linking Peebles and Broughton. Strong walkers may complete the walk in a day, or the route can be split at Stobo. **Length:** 13 miles/21km; *Total Height Climbed:* **1,800ft/560m** (east to west); **1,690ft/515m** (west to east).

O.S. Sheets 72 & 73

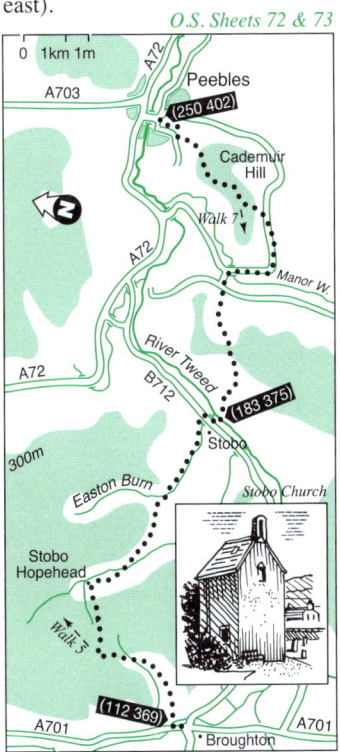

This fine lineal route was established in memory of the author and diplomat John Buchan – best known nowadays as the author of *The Thirty Nine Steps* and other novels. (For more information, visit 'The John Buchan Story', off the High Street in Peebles.)

The map here gives a rough overview of the walk, but the route (although signposted) requires some navigation skills if you are not to get lost in the low hills. Be sure to take OS maps and a compass. A leaflet carrying further information and a description of the route is available at **scotborders.gov.uk**.

At its eastern end, the route technically begins at Bank House on Peebles High Street before crossing the Tweed on the road bridge. It then climbs through the town to reach the first open hills. If you want to avoid the town section, follow the instructions for Walk 7 to reach an alternative start point.

Beyond Cademuir Hill the path descends to a quiet public road, before making a second low hill crossing and descending to the B712 at Stobo, where there is a fine old church. (Stobo is on a regular bus route linking Peebles and Broughton, which can be used to shorten the route.)

The last climb is perhaps the most dramatic: through fine woodland to a low col, before crossing Hopehead Burn and descending through rolling hills by Hollows Burn (*see* Walk 5), passing the fine Broughton Place on the way, to reach the little village of Broughton.

9 Janet's Brae / 10 Peebles & Glentress _____ C/B

9) *A short climb through woodland to a good viewpoint. Length:* **3 miles/5km** (there and back); *Height climbed:* **620ft/190m**. **10)** *An extension of Walk 9: a complex circuit using forest walks and a path/cycle path through woodland and farmland. Length:* **7 miles/11km**; *Height Climbed:* **620ft/190m**.

O.S. Sheet 73

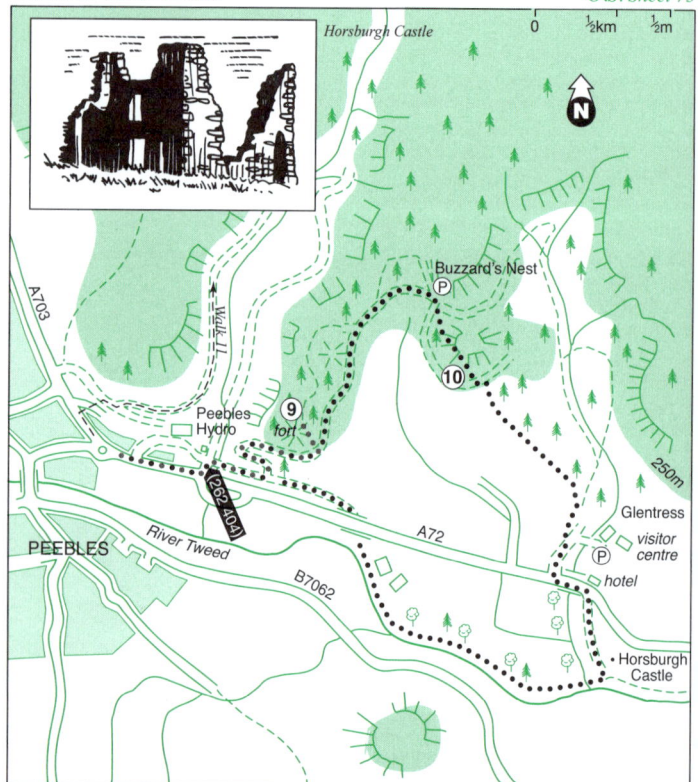

Walks 9 & 10: Walk east from the centre of Peebles on the A72, beyond the roundabout at the junction with the A703. Pass the entrance to the Hydro Hotel and watch for a road to your left, signposted for a cycle route.

After a short distance turn right, onto the cycle track. Follow this through trees, running parallel to and above the road. At the start of the path you pass a sign for the 'Tweed Valley Railway Path'. In a short way you reach two further signs for this walk, on posts in the track. Immediately before these, a rougher track heads off back-left, up the slope.

Take this track, climbing through fine broad-leaved woodland, to a hairpin bend. Double back and continue climbing, still on the main track. Watch for a board to the right of the track, marking the start of the 'Jenny's Brae' community woodland (it is for people coming in the opposite direction, so the writing is on the far side). Immediately beyond this, a fainter path heads off to the left.

Walk 9: Go left here. In a short distance you reach the grassy mounds of an old Iron Age fort, which gives fine views over Peebles and up the valley. Return by the same route.

Walk 10: For the longer route, keep straight on, with fields visible through the fringe of trees to your right. A second track comes in from the left, marked by the number 7 and a green arrow (identifying a cycle route). Keep straight on (also marked by the green arrow, and by a post with a blue ring round it) and continue to the busy Buzzard's Nest car park.

This is the central point for a mass of footpaths and cycle routes through the forest. For this route go right, on the track signposted 'Exit'. After 30 paces go left, on a path. This quickly crosses a second path and continues, marked by a blue post. After a short distance a path marked by a blue/red post goes back left. Keep straight on (red), climbing over the shoulder of a low hill on a rough path.

The path descends to cross a cycle route at an angle then continues (red). Shortly below that you join a vehicle track. Go left along that for 50 paces then go right on a rough path (red). Follow this downhill, with fields visible through the trees to your right. At one point there is a split, with one path continuing by the edge of the trees and the other (red) going left. Follow the red post here (and at subsequent junctions), and you will eventually descend to join a metalled road at an acute angle, just by the Glentress visitor centre, café, etc.

Follow this metalled road down to the A72. Take a few paces to your right to reach the crossing place. Cross (with care) then go left. After 100 paces, directly opposite the Glentress Hotel, a metalled track heads off to the right, signposted for the Tweed Valley Railway Path. Turn down this, noting the ruin of Horsburgh Castle on the hill up to your left.

As you approach the woods by the river there is a T-junction. Turn right here and follow the cycle route, between fields and the woods, for a little over a mile/1.6km to reach the A72. The track passes through a tunnel under the road, then runs beside it to return to the point where you started climbing Janet's Brae. Keep straight on to return to the start.

Walks Peebles, Selkirk & Lanark

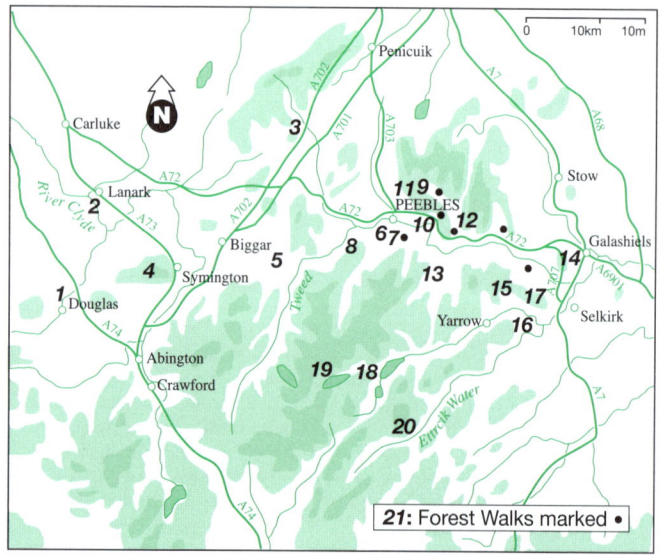

Grades

A ...... Full walking equipment required

B ...... Strong walking footwear and waterproof clothing required

C ...... Comfortable walking footwear recommended

[B/C ...... Split grades mean the route can be walked in shorter sections.]

NB: Assume each walk increases at least one grade in winter conditions. Hill routes can become treacherous.

Walks Peebles, Selkirk & Lanark

	walk	grade
1	Douglas	B
2	Falls of Clyde & New Lanark	B
3	West Linton	A
4	Tinto Hill	B
5	Broughton Heights	A
6	Tweed Walk	B/C
7	Cademuir Hill	B
8	The John Buchan Way	A
9	Janet's Brae	C
10	Peebles & Glentress	B
11	Soonhope Burn	B
12	Lee Pen	B
13	The Glen & Birkscairn Hill	A
14	Meigle Hill	B
15	Minchmoor Road	A
16	Duchess' Drive	B
17	The Three Brethren	B
18	St Mary's Loch	B
19	Broad Law	A
20	Etterick Loop	B
21	Forest Walks	B/C

--- www.pocketwalks.com ---

Published by: *Hallewell Publications, Scotland*
Printed by: *Barr Printers, Glenrothes*

While every care has been taken in the preparation of this guide, the publishers cannot accept responsibility for any loss, damage or injury resulting from its use.

11 Soonhope Burn — B

A short loop from Peebles, climbing one side of a small glen on a clear track then returning down the other side. Paths good throughout.
Length: 3½ miles/5.5km; Height Climbed: 330ft/100m.

O.S. Sheet 73

Park in Peebles and walk to the roundabout at the east end of the main street (the junction of the A703 and the A72). Turn up Edinburgh Road (A703). Pass the car park to your left then cross over to reach a pedestrian ramp leading up from the road.

This climbs to a hairpin bend then doubles back to reach Venlaw Quarry Road. Take a few steps to your right then go left, up a flight of steps. You quickly reach Venlaw High Road. Walk straight across this to reach the start of a rough vehicle track heading up and to the right, into the trees.

Follow this track past the top of a fenced-off quarry. The track then swings left, with the Hydro Hotel visible below. It runs through trees before emerging into farmland and continuing up the side of the glen of Soonhope Burn.

As you approach the buildings at Glenbield there is a signposted junction. The main track goes straight on and an entrance road goes ahead-left. You go right, down a flight of steps.

The path descends to the burn, which it crosses on a small bridge. On the far side, climb a steep slope to join a clear track at a signposted junction. Go right (Peebles) and follow the track down the glen, passing the Soonhope huts – a collection of around 50 small, off-line holiday huts

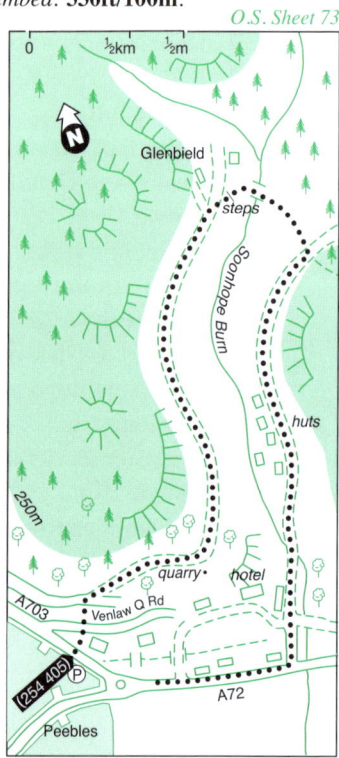

built in a wide variety of styles. The track becomes a metalled road at a line of houses and continues, passing the side entrance to the Hydro then continuing down to the main road.

Turn right to return to the start.

12 Lee Pen _____B

A straightforward climb to a modest peak providing fine views. The path is rough in places but there is little doubt about the route. Length: **4 miles/6.5km** *(there and back); Height Climbed:* **1,170ft/350m**.

O.S. Sheet 73

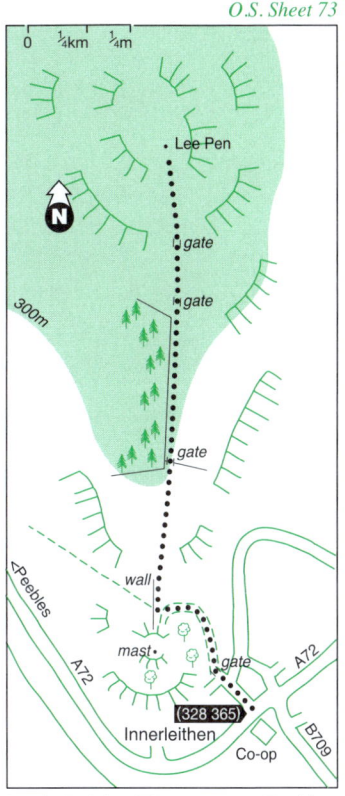

Park in the small town of Innerleithen, 4 miles east of Peebles on the A72, and start walking up St Ronan's Terrace, which turns off the main street directly opposite the Co-op.

When the road swings left, keep straight on. You quickly pass round a wooden gate. Immediately beyond the gate paths head off to right and left. Ignore these and walk straight on, along the clear track.

The track becomes metalled and swings left, up onto a low watershed. At the highest point the track swings left again, leading to radio mast, and there is a wall ahead of you with two gates in it. Ignore these and turn right, with the wall to your left, on a rough path through gorse.

The path climbs to reach a transverse wall with a gate in it, just after a conifer plantation starts to your left. Go through the gate and continue through the field beyond, with the trees to your left. The path is fainter at this stage.

Keep straight on beyond the end of the wood, passing through two further gates in walls before the path leaves the fields and starts to climb steeply up a slope of scree, grass and heather to reach the top. The path is not in any doubt.

There is a fine view from the summit: north along a heathery ridge by the Leithen Water; west to Peebles; and south to Traquair and the hills beyond.

Return by the same route.

13 The Glen & Birkscairn Hill —————————————A

A complex circuit; starting up an estate road through a glen, then climbing to return via an open ridge. Paths faint in places, so some navigation required. Excellent views. Length: **9½ miles/15.5km**; Height Climbed: **1,300ft/390m**.

O.S. Sheet 73

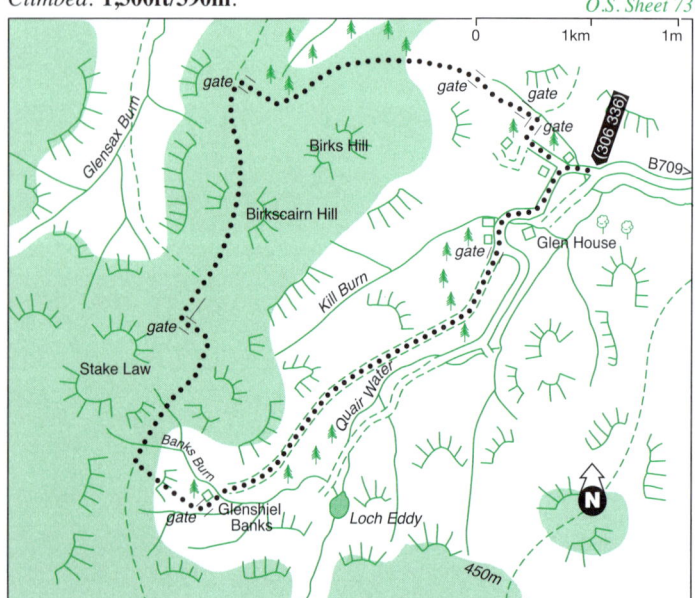

To reach The Glen, drive 2 miles south from Innerleithen (7 miles east of Peebles on the A72) on the B709, then turn right on the minor road signposted for Glen House. A mile along this there is a split, with the entrance to Glen House starting to the left through a stone gateway. At this point there is limited parking to the right of the road. (There is no parking beyond this point, so if it is full you may need to come back later.)

Walk on along the public road. After a short distance there is a signposted junction, with a sign pointing right for Peebles. That is your return route, but for now keep straight on (Glenshiel Banks). A little further on the road passes the splendid 19th-century Glen House, down to your left. Just beyond this it passes a cluster of houses and outbuildings before turning left and passing the farmhouse to your right. Immediately beyond this there is a signposted junction. Go right here (Glenshiel Banks); passing through a gate and continuing along a clear track running up the glen.

Follow this track, through farmland and woodland, for 2 miles/3km to reach the cottage at the track end. Walk past the front of the cottage and keep straight on to reach a gate in a wall. Go through this and turn right, initially with the wall to your right.

The wall bends away, and at this point you will need to do a little navigation. Ahead of you is a slope, with Banks Burn in a shallow glen to your right. Climb the slope parallel to the burn (but far enough to the left to avoid the bracken). Continue up the bank until you are level with the split in the burn to your right, then continue uphill as far again to join a rough, clear path, running across the slope. Turn right along this.

Follow this path across the two burns then up onto the col between the two rounded peaks of Stake Law, with the shallow glen of Kill Burn down to your right. The path then swings left to reach the col between Stake Law and Birkscairn Hill.

The path leads directly to a signposted gate/stile in a fence running along the ridge. Go through the gate and turn right, with the fence to your right (Peebles).

The path and fence lead to the cairn at the top of Birkscairn Hill, then both edge to the left and begin to descend, with Peebles visible ahead through a gap in the hills.

After a little under a mile/1.6km you draw level with the corner of a conifer plantation to your right and there is a signposted gate in the fence. Go through the gate and walk on with a fence – and then the trees – to your left. You quickly reach another corner of the plantation. At this point the trees/fence drop away to your left, but you cross the little Highlandshiels Burn and keep straight on along a rough path contouring the slope of Birks Hill.

The path rejoins the trees at another corner in the plantation. Below the trees you are at the head of a little valley, with a fence to your left. A path goes through this fence, but you ignore this and follow the main track, down the valley.

The fence swings right, across the track, and there is a gate. Immediately beyond this an arrow points left, but for this route keep straight on, through a grazing area. When the track peters out, aim for the left-hand edge of a small wood, visible below.

Just beyond the edge of the trees there is a gate in a fence (arrow). Go through this and follow a grassy path, with the trees to your right and a burn down to your left. After a short distance you reach a signposted junction by a gate to your right.

Go right, through the gate, and follow a clear track through a narrow band of trees. On the far side of the trees you join an access track. Turn left along this to return to the junction passed before.

14 Meigle Hill _____ B

A circuit on rough paths and clear tracks, through woodland and farmland, leading to an excellent hilltop viewpoint. Some care needed with navigation and grazing farm animals along the route. Length: **5 miles/ 8km**; *Height Climbed:* **885ft/270m**.

O.S. Sheet 73

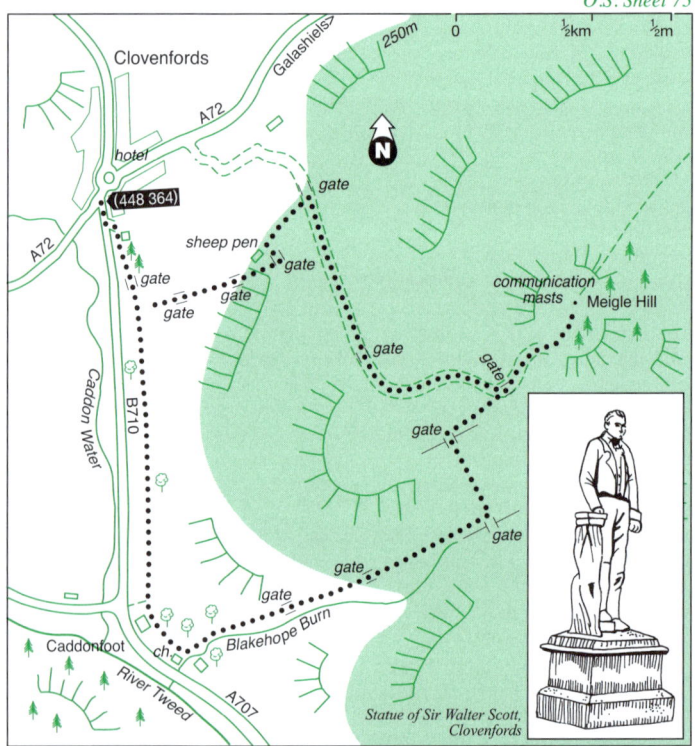

Statue of Sir Walter Scott, Clovenfords

Clovenfords is a small village 2 miles west of Galashiels on the A72, historically famous for its vineyards (founded in 1869 and operated for about 100 years) and for the little coaching inn, with its associations with Sir Walter Scott. To the south of the village is the modest summit of Meigle Hill, topped by communications masts, which provides a good climb and excellent views.

Park in the village and walk south from the roundabout on the A72/Cliff Road. After a short distance, turn left onto Caddonfoot Road. Almost immediately an entrance road starts to your left. Turn on to that, then quickly edge right onto a clear footpath, running through trees with the road down to your right.

The path climbs to the top of the narrow wood, then continues to a gate at the end of the trees. Go through this and continue across the open slope on a clear track, with a fence to your right. After 100 paces you reach a signposted junction. The path to the left is your return route, but for now keep straight on.

Continue on this path for a little under a mile/1.6km. When a path heads right for Caddonfoot, keep straight on, passing a church then swinging to the left, up a wooded glen.

Having left the trees, the path continues across a bank of gorse and bracken until it reaches a gate in a wall. Go through this and enter a field (watch out for cattle from this point on). Continue straight ahead, with the wall down to your right, to reach a second gate. Continue beyond this until you draw level with a gate in the wall to your right, marked by a signpost.

Go left here (Meigle Circular), climbing across the field (no path) to reach a gate just visible in the wall on the far side.

Beyond the gate, turn right (arrow). Follow the wall to your right to reach a gate/cattle grid in a transverse wall, marked by a signpost. Note the track heading back-left on the near side of the wall (Gala Circuit). That is your return route, but for now go through the gate and follow the track beyond as it climbs to the three communications masts, visible ahead.

Once on the peak, take time to walk around (including through the gate in the wall to your right) to get the full view – Galashiels, the Eildon Hills, Selkirk and south to the Cheviot Hills – then double back to the gate/cattle grid and continue down the rough track.

You are now in a large grazing field. Follow the track down to a gate in a wall. Go through this and continue to the next wall/gate, marked by a signpost. Go left on the near side of the wall (Meigle Circular).

There is no clear path at this stage. Just follow the edge of the field to reach a large sheep pen with a shed in it. Turn left on the near side of this (arrow) and a grassy track leads to a gate. Go through this and follow the pen wall to your right. When this ends, head half-right (arrow) to reach a wooden gate in a wall, visible ahead.

Go through this and head straight downhill, with a wall off to your right, descending towards the wooded valley. At the next wall go through one more gate then descend to rejoin your original path at the point noted before.

Retrace your steps to Clovenfords.

15 Minchmoor Road _____A

A moderate circuit, climbing onto an open ridge on rough paths. The views are excellent and there is a possible extension to the Three Brethren cairns (and link with Walk 17). Some care needed with navigation in places. Length: **7½-9 miles/12-14.4km**; *Height Climbed:* **1,200ft/360m**.

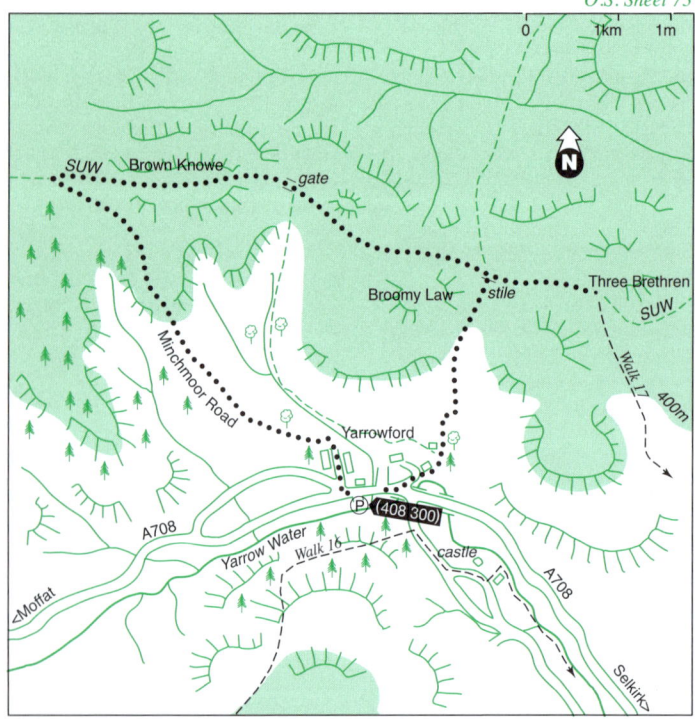

O.S. Sheet 73

Drive 4 miles west from Selkirk on the A708. The road crosses the Yarrow Water and turns sharp left. You are now in Yarrowford. After a short distance there is a phone box to the left of the road, with a space for parking just beyond.

Walk on along the road. After a few paces a road cuts off to the right, signposted for 'The Minchmoor'.

Follow this side road through houses. When the houses end and the road swings left, keep straight on along a clear track for a short distance. Just beyond a playground the track splits. Keep right again. Almost immediately, a sign for the path points left, up steps.

At the top of the steps there is a four-way junction. Keep straight on (yellow arrow), with a wall to your left and rough ground to your right. When the wall pulls away to your left, go through a gate directly ahead and enter a field. Go left (arrow), with the wall to your left and the open field to your right.

Go through a gate in a transverse wall and continue, now with conifers to both sides. At the next wall go right (arrow), with a wall to your left. When the wall ends go through a gate and continue with a fence to your right and trees beyond.

The route now becomes simpler. After a short distance you can see the way clear ahead: a slanting ridge with a wall running up it with conifers to its left. The Minchmoor Road runs up to the left of the wall, before pulling away, through heather and scattered conifers, to reach a signposted junction on the main ridge.

Turn right (Southern Upland Way), climbing to the rounded top of Brown Knowe. Drop down beyond (the views from this ridge are terrific) to a low col, go through a gate in a wall and continue along the top of a wood.

You now have a wall to your right. Follow this through another shallow col then below (ie, to the left of) the peak of Broomy Law. At the next col there is a signposted junction.

If you continue along the ridge (SUW) for a further 3/4 mile/1.2km you will reach the distinctive Three Brethren cairns and link with Walk 17. Otherwise turn right (Yarrowford), crossing a ladder stile.

Immediately beyond the stile there is a gate in a wall to your right. Ignore this and head downhill (watch for a post with an arrow), towards a small glen.

The path flattens out and a field starts to your right, with a gate into it. Ignore this, but join the track which leads up to the gate and follow it down the glen. A wood is visible ahead. When you reach this, cut right, off the track (arrow), and follow a series of duckboards along the top of the wood.

Almost at the end of the wood there is a transverse wall with a gate in it. Go through this. After a few paces there is a second gate to your left. A sign on it tells you to stick to the paths through the woodland beyond.

Go through the gate and follow a pleasant path with a deep glen to your left. When you approach the confluence with the Yarrow the path swings right, with the river at the foot of a steep slope to your left.

Pass a house to your right and walk parallel to its driveway to join the public road. Turn left to join the A708 and turn right (take care on this short stretch) to return to the start.

16 Duchess' Drive _____ B

A waymarked circuit through the grounds of a splendid estate. The route passes through woodland then climbs over the open hill, returning past Newark Castle and along the riverside. Length: **7 miles/11km**; *Height Climbed:* **1,100ft/330m**.

O.S. Sheet 73

Drive 2 miles west from Selkirk on the A708 then turn left at the sign for Bowhill House, the property of the Dukes of Buccleuch. Follow all estate signage for car parking. Access and parking charges apply. (*NB: The following description assumes you are starting from the car park immediately behind the house. At time of writing (2023) the parking for this walk is under review. Please park as the estate indicates.*)

There are four waymarked walks from the car park: two short routes through the grounds in front of the house, a loop by the riverside and a longer circuit climbing onto the open hill. This route makes use of the latter two circuits. A leaflet showing the walks is available in the car park.

Walk on beyond the car park. You quickly pass two forks; keep right (yellow) at both, climbing through mature woodland on a clear track. Beyond this, the route through the trees is difficult to describe but easy to follow: just keep following the signposts until, after a little over a mile/1.6km, you reach a gate in a wall on the edge of the trees.

Once through the gate you are on the open hill. The track starts through grass, crossing a low ridge. Beyond the ridge it joins a stone wall to its right and continues, now through heather, with the slope of Fauldshope Hill to the left. Just before the watershed there is a fork in the track. One keeps to the left of the wall; the other goes right, through a gate. Go right. Beyond the gate the path continues climbing, up onto the ridge.

Once on the ridge you continue, now with a fence to your left with a line of grouse butts set into it. The views from this ridge are splendid.

The path appears to be heading for the peak of Fastheugh Hill, but shortly before you reach it the track goes left, through a gate in the fence. The track now swings round the back of the hill (giving good views into the Yarrow Valley) before going back through the fence.

The path runs parallel to the fence for a short distance before pulling away to the right. Looking ahead-right you will see a distinctive cairn on a hilltop (Newark Hill). A short diversion to the cairn gives a fine view down to Newark Castle. Return to the track and continue.

The track passes back through the fence and descends to a gate on the edge of a conifer plantation. Go through this (arrow). As before, the route is difficult to describe but easy to follow – just follow the arrows at each junction to reach a signposted junction with a metalled road.

Go right. This quiet road quickly swings left and descends to the ruin of Newark Castle: a large tower house originally built for the Douglas family (15th century with later additions).

Just beyond the castle there are buildings to the right of the road. Immediately before, a track heads back left (Lady's Walk). For the quickest return, just continue along the road, but to return by the river take the track to the left, passing behind the cottage at Newark Mill then swinging right to join the riverside path.

The path passes the end of a footbridge. Ignore this and continue, until you reach a split. Go left, down steps, to continue through the trees by the river.

The path eventually pulls away from the river and crosses a metalled road. The path beyond rejoins the entrance drive, shortly before the car park behind the house.

17 The Three Brethren   B

A straightforward hill climb, through woodland and over the open hill, to a well-known landmark and fine viewpoint. Length: **6 miles/9.5km** (there and back); *Height Climbed:* **1,100ft/330m**.

O.S. Sheet 73

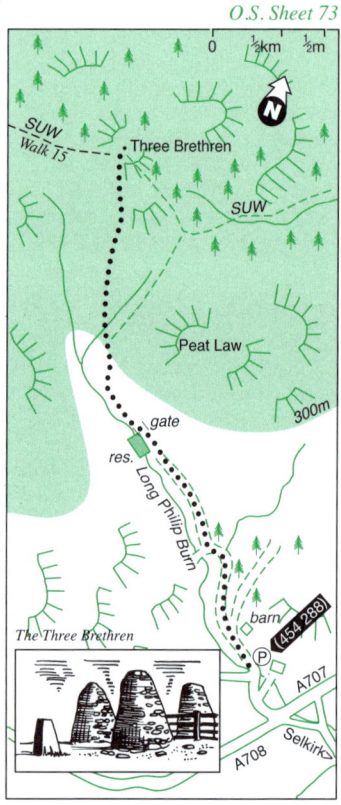

Drive west from Selkirk on the A708. Almost immediately a minor road heads off to your right, marked by a wooden signpost for 'Philiphaugh Walks'. Drive up this road a short way. When the road goes hard left a track goes straight on. Turn onto this track and park to the right.

Continue walking up the track. After a short distance you reach a signposted junction by an old barn. Keep straight on (left), with trees to the right and a field to the left at first, then through conifers with a burn down to your left. Tracks come in from left and right, but you keep straight on (arrows).

The track splits, with the left-hand track crossing the burn. Keep right (arrow) and continue with the burn to your left. Approaching the reservoir a sign marks a path crossing a stile to your left. Ignore this and continue, passing to the right of the reservoir to reach a gate/stile.

Immediately beyond this a path heads right, up the slope. Ignore this and continue on the grassy track by the burn. Continue up this until you reach a signposted fork, with the track going ahead-right and a rougher path going ahead-left. Go left.

Beyond this it is a straightforward climb to the top, where there are wonderful views and a trio of massive cairns – The Three Brethren – built by three landowners to mark the point where their lands met.

Return by the same route.

18 St Mary's Loch — B

A circuit of a loch, through woodland and farmland, following rough paths, tracks and short stretches on the public road. **Length: 7 miles/ 11km**; *Height Climbed: undulating. Keep clear of grazing animals.*

O.S. Sheet 73

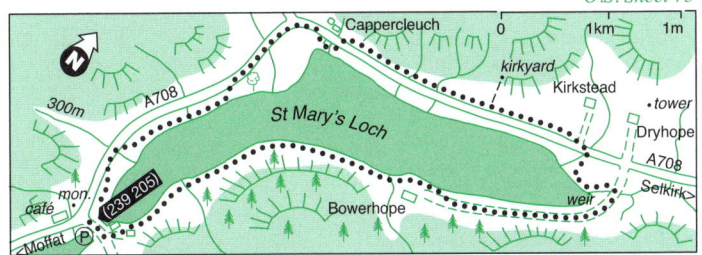

St Mary's is a narrow inland loch, surrounded by hills, about 17 miles south-west of Selkirk on the A708 road to Moffat. Parking is at the west end of the loch, on the flat land between St Mary's and Loch of the Lowes, opposite the Glen Café.

Walk back towards St Mary's (noting the fine monument to the author James Hogg up to your left), then turn right down the minor road which crosses Yarrow Water between the two lochs.

Pass a large white building to your left then turn left into the sailing club. Follow the track round the front of the clubhouse then exit the club grounds by a stile. Beyond this, a faint path (part of the Southern Upland Way) crosses a grazing field above the loch, before continuing through woodland by the lochside.

After 2 miles/3km the path joins the driveway leading into Bowerhope. Continue along this to the end of the loch. Just beyond the bridge over the river, turn left (Ring of the Loch), passing through a pedestrian gate on a metalled track. In a short distance the track ends, by the weir in the river, and you cross a stile into a field.

Walk along the bottom of the field to reach a stile in a wall. Cross this and turn right. Walk up a lane between the wall and a fence to reach the road, by a bridge over a burn.

Cross the road (carefully) and go left for a few paces to reach the entrance to Kirkstead. On the far side of the entrance cross a stile (sign) to enter a field. Walk along the bottom of this long grazing field (keep clear of cattle) for 1½ miles/2.5km until, approaching the first buildings at Cappercleuch, the path drops down to the road.

Follow the signposts – below the buildings, then along the road to cross Megget Water, then on by the shore – to return to the start.

19 Broad Law _____A

A lineal climb up the highest hill in this area. Paths are faint, but there is little doubt about the route – as long as the weather is clear. Length: **5 miles/8km** (there and back); *Height Climbed:* **1,300ft/400m**. *Pick a clear day, to enjoy the views.*

O.S. Sheet 72

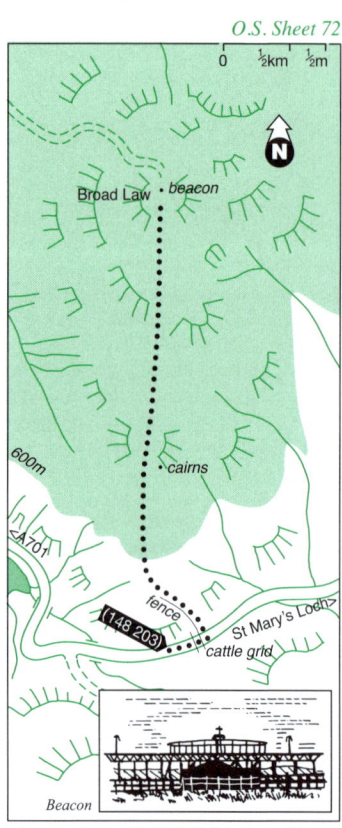

Midway along St Mary's Loch (*see* Walk 18), a minor road heads west from Cappercleuch, passing Megget Reservoir then climbing to a cattle grid at the highest point. Continue for a short distance beyond this to find a parking space to the right of the road. (The west end of this minor road is at Tweedsmuir, on the A701; if you are arriving from this direction, the little road passes Talla Reservoir then makes a steep, winding, narrow ascent beloved of cyclists and motor-cyclists.)

Walk back to the cattle grid and turn left (north) just beyond, climbing on a faint path with a fence to your left.

The path climbs onto a ridge and the fence and path edge right, climbing to the left of two prominent cairns and continuing roughly towards the mast at the top of the hill. The views which gradually open up (as long as you have chosen a clear day) are terrific, with St Mary's Loch down to your right and massive rounded hills in all directions.

Continue shadowing the fence to reach the top of the hill, which is broad, rounded and surprisingly grassy. It is marked by a trig point, two aerials and an unexpectedly sci-fi structure to find in such an isolated place: a large VOR/DME air traffic services beacon.

Return by the same route.

20 Ettrick Loop _____B

A rough hill path over a low watershed (some navigation required), and a return along good tracks and a quiet public road. Length: **5 miles/8km**; *Height Climbed:* **850ft/260m**.

Drive 18 miles south-west from Selkirk on the B7009/B709 to reach the village of Ettrick, then continue west for a short distance on a minor road to reach the car park by the little village hall.

Walk on along the road, passing the monument to James Hogg, to reach the war memorial. Turn right here, up the driveway, passing to the right of the handsome Ettrick Kirk then swinging left, with a burn to your right and buildings to your left.

There is a shed ahead of you with a house beyond. Turn left on the near side of the shed (arrow), climbing on a grassy path through a planted area. After a short distance you reach a gate, beyond which you are on the open hillside.

From this point there is no single path, so you will need to navigate. Pick a quad path and climb up and across the slope, with the Kirk Burn down to your right and the peak of Craig Hill to your left. You climb onto the low col between Craig Hill and Ramsey Knowe then angle down across the slope above Scabcleuch Burn, passing above a round sheep stell.

You will be returning down the Southern Upland Way (visible on the far side of the glen), and your objective is to join this path on the watershed at the top of the burn. Here you should find a fence running across the watershed, and a signpost for the path by a dilapidated stile. Cross this and turn left, along the line of the fence, to reach a gate/stile.

Go left here (SUW) and head down the glen on a clear path. Join the public road opposite Scabcleuch and turn left, along the road, to return to the start.

21 Forest Walks — B/C

Tweed Valley Forest Park is a string of commercial forests, managed by Forestry and Land Scotland. There are six groups of waymarked walks (some touched on in other walks in this guide). A leaflet available at the car parks shows the routes in detail.

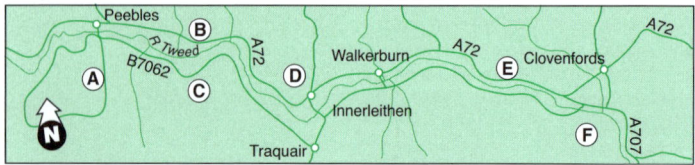

A: Cademuir
The car park for these two routes is just south of Peebles. For instructions on how to reach it, *see* Walk 7.

This is a small plantation, but the height of Cademuir gives good views.

Lengths: **1¼ miles/2.2km; 3¾ miles/6km**

B: Glentress
The main car park for these routes is 2 miles east of the centre of Peebles on the A72. Glentress is best known for its mountain biking routes, but there are also five waymarked walks (*see also* Walk 10) and a café.

Lengths: from **½ mile/0.9km** to **5¾ miles/9.3km.** The routes are linked, to create longer walks.

C: Cardrona
The car park is 3 miles east of the centre of Peebles on the B7062 (ie, to the south of the river).

There are four waymarked walks on good paths through mature woodland; the longest passing an Iron Age fort and giving views over the valley.

Lengths: from **¼ mile/0.3km** to **4 miles/6.6km**

D: Caberston
Turn north from the centre of Innerleithen on Leithen Road (B709) and park in the car park to the right of the road. Walk a short way further up the road to reach the start of this very short walk, climbing through fine woodland to the remains of an Iron Age fort.

Length: **¾ mile/1.4km**

E: Thornielee
The car park is 4 miles east of Innerleithen on the A72. There are two waymarked walks here; the longer climbing **750ft/230m** and providing fine views.

Lengths: **½ mile/1km** and **2½ miles/4.1km**

F: Glenkinnon
6 miles north of Selkirk on the A707, turn south on a minor road signposted for Glenkinnon. Just after crossing the river, the Yair car park is to your left. There is one short walk here, through mixed broadleaf woodland by a small burn.

Length: **1 mile/1.6km**